180 Fun and Challenging Science BrainTeasers for Kids!

SURPRISING SCIENCE

By Nancy De Waard and E. John De W

GoodYearBooks
An Imprint of ScottForesman
A Division of HarperCollinsPublishers

GoodYearBooks

are available for most basic curriculum subjects plus many enrichment areas.
For more GoodYearBooks, contact your local bookseller or educational dealer.
For a complete catalog with information about other GoodYearBooks, please write:

GoodYearBooks
ScottForesman
1900 East Lake Avenue
Glenview, Illinois 60025

ISBN 0-673-36311-2

Printers Code   1 2 3 4 5 6 7 8 - SY - 03 02 01 00 99 98 97 96

Illustration: Tom James. Design: Lynne Grenier.

Ashley and Jack are running through the sprinkler. Water drops are flying every-where. "Look, a rainbow," Jack says to Ashley. What made the rainbow?

The Sahara desert gets 4,300 hours of sun a year—it's the sunniest place on Earth. How many days of sun is that? What fraction of the year is sunny?

SURPRISING SCIENCE

SURPRISING SCIENCE

Air is all around us, even though we can't see it. Air takes up space. What is one way you could show that air takes up space?

On Jupiter things weigh almost three times as much as they do on Earth. On Mars, things weigh only half of what they weigh here. On which planet is gravity strongest? Why?

SURPRISING SCIENCE

Carlos says that drinking milk will give you muscles. Annie says Carlos already has muscles. Who is right?

Leaves are green because of the chlorophyll inside them. But in the fall, leaves change colors. What makes leaves change colors in the fall?

Some insects called water striders can walk on water as easily as you walk on a sidewalk. How can they do this?

Natural sponges come from deep down in the ocean. For many years, people thought sponges were a kind of plant. Now we know this isn't so. What are sponges?

SURPRISING SCIENCE

Do most babies look like their parents? Not always. Some babies have to go through stages before they look like adults. What does a baby butterfly look like?

Darnell was digging in his garden. He accidentally dug into an earthworm and chopped it in two. His dad said the worm would still live. Can an earthworm live if it is chopped in two?

How many ways can you sense sounds? You can hear sound with your ears. You can feel sound too. How can you feel sound?

SURPRISING SCIENCE

If you have a fish tank, one thing that you need to do is place plants in the tank.
Why should you do this?

SURPRISING SCIENCE

Last year, Mr. Brown had many dandelions in his yard. His neighbor, Mr. Green, had none. This spring, Mr. Green's yard has many dandelions. How did the dandelions get to Mr. Green's yard?

Have you ever watched a turtle eat? The mouths of turtles are different from most other animals. How are turtles' mouths different?

Light lets us see. Make a pinhole in the end of a closed shoe box. Peek through the pinhole. Can you see inside the box? What happens if you put a lighted flashlight in the box?

The picture on a color television is made up of tiny dots. The dots are only three colors— red, blue, and green. What makes the other colors?

SURPRISING SCIENCE

Some relatives of the dinosaurs are still living today. One has a very hard shell. Another has sharp teeth and powerful jaws. What are these dinosaur relatives?

SURPRISING SCIENCE

Pine cones can tell you whether the air is damp or dry. How can they do this?

SURPRISING SCIENCE

If you drop an orange and a rubber ball from the same height, which will hit the floor sooner? What force makes things drop to earth?

SURPRISING SCIENCE

Some plants and insects depend on each other. The yucca plant and the yucca moth do. How do yucca plants and yucca moths depend on each other?

Mammals have fur and birds have feathers for protection. What covers butterflies and moths?

People sing because they are happy. But birds sing for a different reason. What is the reason that birds sing?

Mike shows his friends a magic trick. He rubs a balloon on his head and then waves it over some bits of paper. What happens when he does this?

Long ago people used the sun and shadows to tell time. Morning shadows faced west. Afternoon shadows faced east. What time was it when there were no shadows?

SURPRISING SCIENCE

I AM AN INSECT! Don't BUG Me!

Insects form the largest group of living things on Earth. Over one million species have been identified, and there probably are many more. How can you identify an insect?

SURPRISING SCIENCE

Your tongue has two different senses. You can taste sweet, sour, and salty things with your tongue. What other sense does your tongue have?

Insects have skeletons on the outside of their bodies called exoskeletons. What supports your body?

Animals that hunt other animals for food are called predators. Predators have eyes on the front of their faces. Most prey animals have eyes on the sides of their faces. Is a rabbit a predator?

If you put your hand in front of your face, you can feel your breath. When the air is cold, you can see your breath. What makes it possible to see your breath when it's cold?

SURPRISING SCIENCE

Most plants need soil to grow. But many plants can be grown without soil. How can you grow plants without soil?

If you took a spaceship to an alien planet, you would need three things to survive. What would you need?

Molds are organisms that grow from spores. You may have seen a green mold growing on bread or fruit. What important medicine comes from mold?

SURPRISING SCIENCE

Make a parachute. Tie one piece of string to each corner of a handkerchief. Tie a weight at the ends of the strings. Toss the parachute into the air. Why doesn't it fall quickly?

An octopus is an animal that lives in the sea. It has long arms and many suckers on each arm. The suckers help the octopus catch its food. How many arms does an octopus have?

Sarah is showing her rock collection. Some rocks are very rough. Others are smooth. Jim says the smooth rocks came from a beach. How does he know this?

Peter and Emalee made a sand castle by mixing sand and water together and forming towers and walls. Later, the sand castle fell apart. What happened that made the castle fall?

An animal lives under the porch at Katie's house. It has two big flat front teeth, small ears, and fur that is grayish-brown. Does this animal eat meat? What could the animal be?

Bones are different for different animals. The bones of a hummingbird are not like the bones of an elephant. Why are hummingbird bones different than elephant bones?

Even though snakes have no legs or feet, they can swim and climb trees as well as animals with feet. Are snakes mammals or reptiles?

Lin and Zack went sledding. Later the sun melted the snow a bit. The next day their sleds went very fast. Why did their sleds go faster?

Soak a bean seed in water for a day. Then peel off the skin and open the seed. Look for the tiny sprout. A magnifying glass helps. How many parts does a bean seed have?

SURPRISING SCIENCE

Have you ever seen a volcano? Melted rock and steam pour out of a volcano. Ashes make the sky dark. What is melted rock from a volcano called?

SURPRISING SCIENCE

How are a watch dog and a maple tree alike?

Have you lost some of your baby teeth? New teeth grow in their place. Teeth are needed for chewing and talking. You have four kinds of teeth. What are the four kinds of teeth?

SURPRISING SCIENCE

Take two balloons, one blown up and one deflated, and tape one to each end of a ruler. Tie a string around the center of the ruler and pick up the ruler by the string. Which side is heavier? What does this show?

SURPRISING SCIENCE

Animals and insects do not see the way that people do. Their eyes are different from ours. Grasshoppers have five eyes! How are insect eyes different from people's eyes?

SURPRISING SCIENCE

Daniel went to his brother's basketball game. He wanted his brother to hear his cheering. So he cupped his hands around his mouth. Will this really help?

Dolphins are amazing animals. They seem to talk to each other. Dolphins have even learned to help people. How have dolphins helped people?

SURPRISING SCIENCE

Your tooth fell out! You put it under your pillow. In the morning you found a dollar and a note that says, "Drink three glasses of milk every day." Why is this good advice?

Some kinds of insects live together. Bees, ants, wasps, and termites live in groups. Many of these insects build homes. What materials do wasps use for their homes?

SURPRISING SCIENCE

Rub your hands together. After a while you will probably feel heat. Why do your hands feel very warm after rubbing?

SURPRISING SCIENCE

Your ears tell you a lot about the world around you. You can sometimes tell what is going on just by hearing sounds. Have a friend make a sound. Can you guess what the sound was?

Fish live underwater but they need to breathe oxygen just like you. How do fish breathe?

Long ago, people found that water could help do hard work. Fast moving rivers were good places to build factories. How did water help do work?

Keesha and Sam want to move a large box. It's too big to carry or drag, but Keesha thinks of an easy way to move it. What would be an easy way to move the box?

At the North and South poles of the Earth, there is always snow and ice—even in the summertime. What is the reason that the snow never melts at the poles?

SURPRISING SCIENCE

Energy is what makes things move or get warm. Have you heard of "burning energy" when you play? What does "burning energy" mean?

Jamal went fishing and fell into the creek. His father laid Jamal's wet clothes on a bush. Thirty minutes later they were dry. What happened to the water?

SURPRISING SCIENCE

Stir salt into a cup of water. Tie one end of a string to a paper clip and the other end around a pen. Place the pen across the cup and let the paper clip hang in the water for a few days. What do you see on the string?

Many animals have spots and stripes in their fur. Some insects look just like leaves or sticks. How does this camouflage help living things survive?

SURPRISING SCIENCE

What is black and white and red all over? A zebra with a sunburn. How can the sun burn your skin?

If you watch the night sky in the summertime, you may see a falling star. Do stars really fall out of the sky?

One of the oldest plants on Earth is moss. You can find moss growing anywhere there is shade and moisture. How do scientists know moss is an old plant?

HOME OF MR. P. MOSS

SURPRISING SCIENCE

Fireflies are sometimes called lightning bugs. But they aren't flies or bugs. What are they?

Richard says that he is a red-blooded American. Tasha says that red blood has nothing to do with being an American. What gives blood its color?

SURPRISING SCIENCE

A green plant will grow toward light. You can see this for yourself. Cut a window in a cardboard box. Plant some radish seeds in a pot and cover it with the box. What happens?

Kim asked her grandfather, "Why is the moon round tonight?" "The moon is always round," he said. "Sometimes, we just can't see all of it." Why can't we always see all of the moon?

Silk is a very beautiful fabric. It is called a natural fiber because its thread is not made by humans. How is silk made?

SURPRISING SCIENCE

Can sunlight heat water? Think of how you might find an answer to this question. Try your idea. What did you find out?

SURPRISING SCIENCE

The Earth and all the planets travel around the sun. Does the moon travel around the sun too?

Dinosaurs lived millions of years ago. Many of them were very, very large. Were dinosaurs the biggest animals that have ever lived?

Birds and many reptiles lay eggs. Most birds build nests, but reptiles often dig holes in the soil for their eggs. How are reptiles' eggs kept warm?

Exercise, such as running and jumping, is good for you. How is running and jumping good for you?

Whistling tea kettles tell you when the water in the kettle is boiling. What makes the tea kettle whistle?

Camels can store enough water in their bodies to last for several days. Why is it important for camels to be able to store water?

If you have ever seen pictures of a shark, you probably remember its long, sharp teeth. Sharks' teeth are unusual. How are sharks' teeth different from other animals' teeth?

All living things can be grouped. Plants that have thick woody stems and grow tall are grouped as trees. What group of animals have scales and fins and live in water?

Once people believed that the sun and all the planets traveled around the Earth. How did they find out the sun was at the center?

Wasps are insects that build their own homes. Wasp homes are called nests. The nests can be made of paper or mud. Are wasps and bees the same kind of insect?

Cody and Thomas were playing with toy cars. They built a ramp and raced the cars down it. What force made the cars roll down the ramp?

SURPRISING SCIENCE

Long ago, people thought the earth was flat. Some thought you could sail off the edge of the earth. Why can't you sail off the edge of the earth?

SURPRISING SCIENCE

140 LEVEL 1

Not all butterflies hatch from cocoons. Some butterflies, such as monarchs, hatch from a pupa. What is the difference between a cocoon and a pupa?

DO NOT DISTURB

You can tell a lot about an animal by looking at its feet. What could you tell about an animal with webbed feet?

Weather is important to people. Sunshine and rain are important for growing food. Some things we do are harmful to weather. What is smog?

SURPRISING SCIENCE

When you take a picture with a camera, you need to have light. Why do you need light?

As you grow, your bones get longer and your skin gets larger. Animals such as snakes grow differently. When they grow, they burst out of their skins. Why do snakes grow in this way?

Most plants have green leaves and need sunlight. What will happen if a plant does not get sunlight?

Scoo...bee...
doo...bee-doo

Many animals sing. They always sing the same song over and over. Their song tells who they are. What animal changes its song from year to year?

Magnets are fun. They are also useful. They can push and pull other magnets and certain metals. How do magnets push or pull?

Long ago, sailors believed that monsters lived in the sea. It is true that many large creatures live in oceans. What mammal is almost as large as a small whale?

Animals are able to move around, which helps them protect themselves. Plants cannot protect themselves in this way. How do some plants protect themselves?

Brad found a green tree toad. He put the toad into a box. When he opened the box, the green toad was gone. A gray toad was in the box! Where is the green toad?

TONY
the Amazing
TOAD ☆

SURPRISING SCIENCE

Plants cannot move from place to place as animals do. But plants do move over time. How can plants move from place to place?

Everyone knows that a red light means stop and a green light means go. Do you know why traffic lights are red and green and not blue and purple?

SURPRISING SCIENCE

48 LEVEL 1

Most animals are very small when they are born. Opossums are so tiny that three babies would fit in a teaspoon! Where do baby opossums hide until they are big?

Dragonflies have been on the Earth for 300 million years! Their wings beat 1,600 times a minute—you can't see them move! They are great hunters. What do dragonflies hunt?

Water falls from the clouds as rain, hail, or snow. How does water get into the clouds?

CLOUDS or BUST!

There are many different climates in the world. Some people live in cold climates. Some live in hot climates. Many live in climates with seasons. What kind of climate do you live in?

SURPRISING SCIENCE

On a hot day, the lifeguard at the pool where José swims sprays the walk around the pool with water. Why does he do this?

Almost all living things need sunlight to live. Deep in the ocean, there is no sunlight. Yet many animals live there. How do they live without sunlight?

SURPRISING SCIENCE

Air pushes in on your body and on everything around you. What happens when air pushes in on an object?

Electricity is powerful energy. Did you know that there are 500 kinds of fish that make electricity? Electric eels are one of these. How much electricity can an electric eel produce?

We use energy every day, breathing, digesting food, and moving. What uses the most energy: cleaning your room, watching TV, or riding your bike?

Nothing travels faster than light. Light can travel from the moon in 1.3 seconds. The distance to the moon is 384,000 kilometers. If you could walk to the moon, how long would it take?

TO THE MOON →

Juanell stirred 2 spoons of salt into 2 spoons of hot water. Then she wrote a message in this invisible ink. In 30 minutes the message disappeared. How could you read the message later?

A praying mantis is a good helper to have in your garden. Some garden companies sell egg cases of the praying mantis. What makes the mantis so helpful?

SURPRISING SCIENCE

Maple seeds have wings that make the seeds whirl as they fall. What causes the seeds to whirl? Why would this be an important feature in a seed?

You can use a lever to do many kinds of work. A lever can help you lift or push something large. Which of these items is a lever—a pair of scissors, a hammer, or a wheelbarrow?

SURPRISING SCIENCE

Honey bees can't talk, but they can tell other bees where to find flowers and nectar. How do they do this?

Some kinds of sharks are very dangerous to people and other animals. Sharks do not have bones as other animals do. What do sharks have in place of bones?

The moon looks like a giant orange pumpkin coming up behind the trees. But as it gets higher in the sky, it looks smaller. Why do you think the moon looks so large when it is rising?

People have always wished they could talk to animals. However, people have learned to talk to chimpanzees. How can people talk to chimpanzees?

SURPRISING SCIENCE

Leaves have different shapes. You probably know what maple leaves look like. Look at other kinds of leaves. How could you show different shapes of leaves?

Do plants always grow from seeds? Some plants, such as African violets, ivy, and coleus, are easier to grow from cuttings. How can you grow plants from cuttings?

Elephants have been around for 58 million years. The first elephants were the size of pigs. They were only about two feet tall. How big was the biggest elephant that ever lived?

SURPRISING SCIENCE

There are several different kinds of kangaroos. The largest may weigh up to 200 pounds and be seven feet tall. How small is the smallest kangaroo?

SURPRISING SCIENCE

The first space capsule was called *Sputnik*. It was launched in 1959 by the former Soviet Union. Who was the first American in space?

SURPRISING SCIENCE

SURPRISING SCIENCE

122 LEVEL 1

James lives on a farm. He raises chickens and ducks. He also has a pet kitten and calf. The kitten and calf drink their mother's milk. What are animals that drink milk from their mothers called?

Animals can't talk, but they do communicate. If your cat purrs and rubs against you, it's happy to see you. What does it mean when your cat arches its back and spits?

Mercury is the planet closest to the sun. A year on Mercury is 88 days long. Would you be older or younger if you lived on Mercury?

Some insects, such as grasshoppers, shed their skins each time they grow larger. Why must grasshoppers shed their skins to grow?

OLD SKIN

SURPRISING SCIENCE

Rocks and minerals are all around you. They are used in many different ways. How can you tell a rock from a mineral?

Plants perspire just as you do in the summertime. Water vapor escapes through tiny holes in the leaves. How can you prove that plants perspire?

Grass is one of the most common plants in the world. It grows everywhere. There are many kinds of grass that are important foods for people! What kinds of grass are foods for people?

GRASSIOS

SURPRISING SCIENCE

The Earth is always moving. It moves in two ways. It spins like a top, and as it spins, it moves around the sun. How can you tell that the Earth is moving?

Have you ever watched two kittens playing? One kitten may jump out at another. Sometimes they creep up on each other. This kind of play is very important. Why?

A barometer is an instrument used to measure air pressure. Have you heard a meteorologist say, "The barometer is falling"? What does this mean?

Have you ever played on a seesaw? Seesaws are like a balance. You can move the seesaw or yourself to make it balance. How can you balance a seesaw if your friend is heavier than you?

SURPRISING SCIENCE

Mars is often called the "red planet." When *Voyager* landed on Mars, it sent back pictures proving the soil of Mars is red. If an astronaut on Mars looked at Earth, what color would she see?

Microbes are very tiny living things. Some cause disease. But others help to break down dead plants and animals. What would happen if microbes didn't break down dead materials?

Tyrone does not like to eat vegetables. But his mother says vegetables are good for him. Why should Tyrone eat his vegetables?

SURPRISING SCIENCE

Tony and Julio made a telephone. They used string and paper cups. How do paper cups and string carry a message?

Rockets fly because of gasses pushing them. The gasses push as they rush out of the back of the rocket. In what direction does the rocket move?

Jeremy says he is having roots, seeds, and berries for lunch! If he offers to share with you, what do you think you might have to eat?

Some animals have special patterns of spots, stripes, or colors in their fur. How do these patterns help them survive?

Warm air rises and cold air sinks. You can show this. Hold a balloon over a lighted lamp. Let it go. Does the balloon rise or sink?

Everyone knows that most birds fly. But some animals "fly" too. Have you heard of flying foxes or flying squirrels? How do these animals "fly"?

Trees can live a long time. How long? Some oaks and maple trees can live to be 200 years old. How can you tell how old a tree is?

SURPRISING SCIENCE

You can bend your elbow, sit down, and wiggle your toes because you have joints. How many joints do you have in your body?

Wind can do work for us. Have you seen windmills? They are used for pumping water out of the ground and grinding grain. How does wind power a windmill?

How is a goldfish like your bathroom?

SURPRISING SCIENCE

Some flowers bloom only at night. Often these flowers are light-colored or white. Night-bloomers are sometimes fragrant. How do the colors and smells help these flowers?

PERFUME

SURPRISING SCIENCE

Most plants make their own food. But some plants trap insects as well. What plants trap insects?

Earthworms are important animals. Why? It's not because they are sometimes used for fish bait. How are earthworms important?

Michael shows Lateesha a trick. He sucks lemonade into his straw. Then he covers the top of the straw with his finger and pulls it out of the lemonade. What will happen?

SURPRISING SCIENCE

Spiders live almost everywhere. Many of them spin webs that trap insects. Are spiders insects?

Try this. Fill a bowl with water. Push the open end of a glass straight down into the water. Only a little water will go into the glass. What is keeping the water out?

Many people are afraid of bees and wasps because they sting. They forget that these insects are very important to people. How do bees and wasps help people?

Electricity can attract water. Try combing your hair several times. Then hold your comb beside some running water. What happens?

Animals such as lizards, toads, and snakes are called "cold-blooded." To get warm, they need a warm place. To cool off, they need a cool place. How do snakes survive in the desert?

Pints, liters, and quarts are ways that we measure fluids. What are some ways to measure distance?

Friction can be a problem in machines such as bicycles. Friction causes heat and wear on metal parts. What can you do to reduce friction?

The water in the ocean is salty. The water in lakes is not salty and can freeze in the winter. Will saltwater freeze?

Patrick was getting a checkup from his doctor. The doctor listened to Patrick's heart with a stethoscope. How does a stethoscope help the doctor listen?

THUMPA THUMPA THUMP

Butterflies and moths look very much alike. But there are ways to tell them apart. How can you tell a moth from a butterfly?

SURPRISING SCIENCE

The air around us has moisture. Fill a plastic cup with ice cubes. Pour water over the ice. Add a few drops of food color. Later check the outside of the cup. What has happened?

Turtles have been on Earth for millions of years. Even long ago, turtles had shells much like the turtles you know. The biggest turtle that ever lived was Archelon. How big was Archelon?

Some birds do not fly. The penguin is one of these. Most penguins live near oceans and catch fish and squid. How do they catch fish?

Electricity is an important kind of energy. It makes the lights in your house glow. It runs the TV, the toaster, and many other things. When have you seen electricity in nature?

Frogs and toads lay their eggs in water. The eggs have little black specks instead of yolks. They do not have shells! How can you tell if eggs you have found are frog eggs or toad eggs?

Some kinds of insects live together in groups. They have a queen and many workers. Bees are insects that live like this. What is another insect that lives in a group?

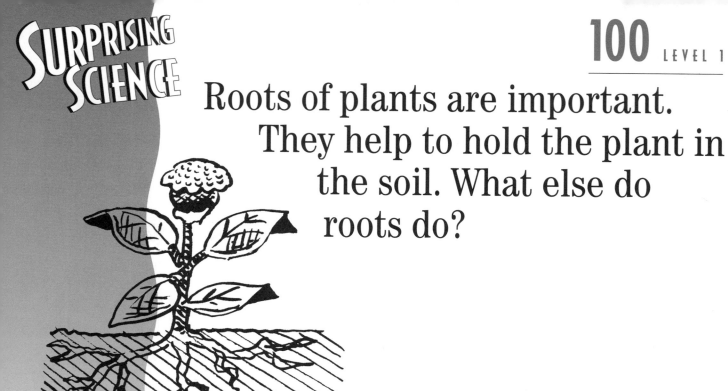

Roots of plants are important. They help to hold the plant in the soil. What else do roots do?

Some things that look like insects are really not insects. An Li found something under a pile of leaves. It looked like a caterpillar, but it had many little legs. It moved very quickly. What was this animal?

You can make a musical instrument. Collect several sizes of rubber bands. Stretch them across a shoe box and strum them. What causes the rubber bands to make different sounds?

SURPRISING SCIENCE

An air-filled bottle will float. Sometimes people put messages in bottles and throw them into the sea. It's fun to wait for someone to find the message. What happens if you add a little water to the bottle?

SURPRISING SCIENCE

Long ago people thought sickness was caused by evil spirits. Now we know that germs cause illness. How does your body fight diseases?

Most birds are smaller than people. They need to be small and light so they can fly. What is the largest bird?

Water is important to all living things. We need to use water carefully. How can you use water carefully?

Frogs and toads can live in water and on land. Both frogs and toads lay their eggs in water where they hatch. What are animals that can live on water or land called?

Plants need light like we need food. Plants use light to make food. What happens if you turn a plant away from a window it has been facing?

SURPRISING SCIENCE

Marco is petting his kitten's fur. Suddenly, he hears a crackling sound and feels a shock. His kitten's fur is standing straight up. What caused the crackling sound and the shock?

The sky looks blue. So do lakes and oceans. Have you ever wondered why? Fill a clear bottle with water and a few drops of milk. Darken the room. Shine a light through the bottle. What do you see?

The largest plant in the world is a redwood tree called the General Sherman Tree. It is 101 feet 7 inches around at the base. It is 274 feet 7 inches high. What is the smallest plant in the world?

Angie tells Mark she can move a sheet of paper on the table without touching it. How can she do it? What moves the paper?

Do you have a Boston fern at your house? Ferns do not have flowers or seeds. How do ferns spread?

SURPRISING SCIENCE

Your heart will beat more than two billion times in your lifetime. What does your heart do to keep you healthy?

SURPRISING SCIENCE

Cats and some other kinds of animals can see in the dark. How can they do this?

SURPRISING SCIENCE

The largest seed in the world weighs up to 40 pounds. It takes six years to ripen. What is the largest seed in the world?

Hot air rises. Long ago, someone thought of a way of using hot air to travel in the sky.
How can people use hot air to travel above the Earth?

SURPRISING SCIENCE

David's mom bought vegetables that looked like large green pine cones. She told him they were artichokes. When David eats an artichoke, what part of the plant will he be eating?

SURPRISING SCIENCE

1: Light shining through water drops is refracted (separated) into colors in the same way as when light shines through a glass prism. The colors that make up the white sunlight are bent by different amounts as they pass through the drops. This process separates the colors so you can see them.

2: Blow up a balloon or puff out your cheeks.

3: Everyone is born with muscles, but a nutritious diet, including milk, helps keep your muscles strong.

4: Water has a kind of skin, called surface tension, on which the water strider can walk.

5: A baby butterfly is a caterpillar. Even tiny butterflies are adults.

6: Put your ear on a table. Hit the table. This makes a sound and you can feel the vibrations. Or turn up your stereo and feel the floor thump. (Don't do this for long!)

7: The wind carried the dandelions seeds from Mr. Brown's yard to Mr. Green's. Every summer and fall you can see dandelion seeds as their "parachutes" carry them on the wind.

8: You cannot see inside the box without light.

9: Turtles; crocodiles and alligators

10: They will both hit at the same time. Gravity, which is the pull of the earth, makes them fall.

11: Butterflies and moths are covered with colored scales.

12: The balloon is charged with static electricity from Mike's hair. If it is a dry day, the paper will jump to the balloon.

13: Insects have six legs, three body parts, and, usually, two pairs of wings.

14: Your body is supported by a skeleton of bones inside (an endoskeleton).

15: The cold air causes the water in your breath to condense, forming a tiny cloud.

16: Food, water, and air

17: Air pushes up against the parachute and slows it as gravity pulls it down.

18: Most small stones are pieces that have broken off larger ones. These pieces are rough. Water rolling the stones back and forth has made them smooth.

19: No, if the animal was a meat eater, it would have sharp, pointed teeth. This animal is probably a woodchuck and eats grass and other plants.

20: Snakes are reptiles.

21: Bean seeds are dicots. There will be two distinct halves to their seeds. Most of what you see is food for the baby plant. With a magnifying glass you can see the tiny plant with its two seed leaves (cotyledons).

22: They both are protected by barks.

23: The blown-up balloon is heavier; air has weight.

24: Yes, it will. Sound travels in waves that spread out. By cupping his hands around his mouth, Daniel is concentrating the sound.

25: Milk has calcium. You need calcium for strong bones and healthy teeth.

26: As you rub your hands together, you are creating friction. Friction happens anytime things rub together. Friction changes the motion energy of your hands to heat energy.

27: Fish take in water through their mouths and pass it over their gills. Oxygen is dissolved in the water. The gills collect the oxygen from the water.

28: Put the box on something that will roll. Rolling friction is much less than sliding friction.

29: Burning energy means using up the energy you get from your food. You are burning energy when you move, talk, breathe, or even digest food.

30: Salt crystals

31: The ultraviolet rays in sunlight burn your skin. Your eyes can't see the ultraviolet rays, but they are the most dangerous rays in sunlight.

32: They have found fossils of mosses in very old rocks. Mosses have no true roots, stems, or leaves.

33: Blood is red because of red blood cells. The red cells contain iron, which is red, and helps to carry oxygen from the lungs.

34: We see the moon because sunlight reflects off it. Sometimes, as the moon moves around the Earth, the Earth blocks some of the sunlight. Then the moon does not look round.

35: Yes, sunlight can heat water.

36: No. They may have been the biggest animals on land, but blue whales are the biggest animals that have ever lived. A blue whale can be 100 feet long and weigh 130 tons.

37: Exercise keeps your muscles, joints, and other body systems in top shape.

Exercise is good for your heart muscles and lungs too.

38: Camels are desert animals. Sometimes they must go for many days before they can find a drink.

39: They are fish.

40: No. They are both insects, but different species. Bees nests are made of wax and contain combs that store honey and protect their young. Wasps do not make honey.

41: The earth is round and gravity keeps everything on earth from escaping.

42: Animals with webbed feet spend a lot of time in water.

43: The rays of sunlight interact with chemicals on the film that make the picture. This is why photographs must be developed in the dark or under special lights that do not affect the film.

44: The plant turns yellow and brown because it needs the light to produce its green color.

45: The poles of a magnet attract (pull) or repel (push) other magnets and some metals, especially those containing iron.

46: Plants such as cactus have sharp thorns. Trees have hard trunks covered with bark. Can you think of other ways plants protect themselves?

47: The seeds of plants travel by wind, by water, and by being carried by animals.

48: Opossums live in a pouch on their mother's body for two months until they are large enough to explore the world outside.

49: By evaporation. Water vapor in the air travels upward and condenses into clouds. When conditions are right, the water falls as rain or snow.

50: To cool the pavement. As the water evaporates, it absorbs heat energy and cools the pavement. This allows people to walk around the pool without burning their feet.

51: If the pressure inside is the same, nothing happens. However, if the pressure inside is less, the object will be squeezed.

52: Riding your bike. The more large-muscle groups you use at once, and the harder you work, the more energy you use.

53: The water will evaporate, but tiny bits of salt are left on the paper. If you rub the paper lightly with a pencil, the salty writing will appear.

54: The air, flowing past the wings, makes them whirl round and round.

The wind can carry the seeds farther from the tree than if they just dropped to the ground. There is a better chance that some seeds will make it to good soil where they can grow.

55: Honey bees talk to each other by dancing. A circular dance means that nectar is close by. A dance that follows a figure-8 pattern means the nectar is farther away.

56: One theory is that the rising moon looks large because you see it behind trees and buildings and, in comparison, it looks larger.

57: You can do two things. You can make leaf rubbings by placing a leaf wrong side up under a sheet of paper. With a crayon, rub gently over the paper. The shape of the leaf will appear. You can press fresh leaves by placing them in an old telephone book and letting them dry. Then mount them on paper and identify them. You can make a book!

58: The largest of all elephants was the woolly mammoth. It was about 11 feet tall at the shoulder, and its tusks were about 15 feet long. Mammoths became extinct about ten thousand years ago.

59: The first American astronaut was Alan Shepard who was rocketed into space May 5, 1961.

60: Your cat is showing you that she's frightened or angry. Animals use body language and noise to tell what they feel.

61: Grasshoppers' skeletons are on the outside of their bodies. Because this exoskeleton is stiff and cannot stretch, it must be shed before the grasshopper can grow larger.

62: Place a glass jar or plastic bag over a potted plant in a sunny place. Do not add water to the plant. Check the inside surface of the container after an hour.

63: You can see how the sun seems to move from east to west. The Earth is actually moving around the sun.

64: It means that the air pressure is getting lower. This probably means that a storm is coming.

65: The planet Earth would look blue because of its water and air. You can see this in the photos taken from the moon.

66: Vegetables have carbohydrates, vitamins, and minerals that help him grow strong.

67: The rocket moves in the opposite direction of the gasses. As most rockets are pointed upward, they move toward the sky.

68: Most animals do not see colors, only black, white, and gray. Spots, stripes, and colors help the animal to hide from enemies.

69: Flying foxes are large bats that look a bit like foxes. They fly using their wings, just like other bats. Flying squirrels don't really fly. They use a wide flap of skin between their legs to glide from tree to tree.

70: There are sixty-eight joints in your body. See if you can find them all! (Don't forget your fingers and toes!)

71: They both have scales.

72: Venus flytrap and pitcher plants both trap insects. These plants grow in bogs. The insects give them minerals that they need to grow and can't get from the acid water in the bogs.

73: The lemonade that is in the straw stays there. Air pushing up keeps it there. If Michael takes his finger off the straw, air pressure will act on the top and the lemonade will drain out.

74: There is air in the glass. The water pushes the air into the space at the top of the glass. Tilt the glass slightly to the side and see what happens.

75: By combing your hair, you have given your comb an electric charge. The water is attracted and will bend toward the comb.

76: Meters, kilometers, inches, feet, and miles are measures of distance.

77: Yes, but at much lower temperatures than fresh water.

78: Moths have feathery antennae and usually fly at night. Butterflies have knobbed antennae and fly during the day. When moths rest, they spread their wings flat. Butterflies keep their wings pointed up.

79: Archelon was 11 feet long and 12 feet wide. This turtle lived in the ancient sea.

80: You have probably seen lightning in a thunderstorm. This is electricity that builds up in clouds.

81: Ants and termites live in groups too.

82: It was a centipede. Centipedes are not worms or insects. They belong to a group of animals called chilopods (key-lo-pods).

83: It will still float, but your message will get soggy! If you add too much water, the bottle will sink.

84: The African ostrich is the largest bird. It can be up to 9 feet tall and weigh up to 345 pounds! Ostriches don't fly, but they can run up to 35 miles per hour.

85: Animals that live on water and on land are called amphibians.

86: The crackling sound and the shock are caused by static electricity. When you shuffle across a carpet on a cool, dry day, you will pick up some electricity. If you reach out to a doorknob or other metal. You may get a shock.

87: You may have seen the smallest plant in the world growing on a pond. It is called duckweed. Its flower is only ⅛ of an inch wide.

88: Ferns spread by spores. If you turn over a fern leaf, you may see little brown specs that look like seeds. Hold a paper under the leaf. Shake it gently. Do you see brown dust? These are spores that can grow new ferns.

89: If you have a cat, look at the shape of its pupils. Your pupils are round but your cat's are oval. The cat's pupils can open wide at night to pick up more light. They can close to a slit in daylight to shut out bright light.

90: Hot air balloons lift passengers above the earth.

91: Artichokes are flower buds.

92: The largest seed in the world is the seed of a double coconut palm tree.

93: The heart pumps blood to all parts of your body. This carries food and oxygen to all of your cells.

94: She blows on the paper. The moving air of her breath moves the paper.

95: White light has all the colors of the rainbow. But small particles, such as dust and milk drops, bend the color blue most. So this color shows more.

96: The plant will slowly turn its leaves to face the window and the light. This is called heliotropism.

97: Do not waste water by letting the faucet run. Take short showers. Store water in the refrigerator to keep it cold. Water your lawn in the afternoon or evening when there will not be much evaporation.

98: Your skin protects against some germs. So do white blood cells in your blood. Shots from your doctor can also prevent disease. Your body develops immunity when you receive a shot.

99: The rubber bands are of different thicknesses, lengths, and tensions. These differences make each band vibrate differently.

100: They carry water and food from the soil into the plant.

101:   Frog eggs are found in clumps. Toads lay their eggs in strings.

102:   Penguins' wings have turned into flippers. They use their flippers to swim fast and catch the fish and squid.

103:   The cup looks as though it's sweating. You can tell the water did not leak out of the cup because it's clear, but you colored the cup's water. When warm air comes in contact with the cold cup, the moisture in the air condenses on the cup.

104:   The stethoscope concentrates the sound. This helps the doctor clearly hear the sound waves the heart makes when it is pumping blood. It can also help the doctor hear the sound of your lungs breathing.

105:   You can make the parts that move against each other very slippery. Oil is slippery. That's why we add oil to the parts of a bike and the engine in a car.

106:   They warm themselves in the morn-ing sun. Then they find a cool burrow underground when the sun is hot.

107:   These insects are important to us because they pollinate many plants. If bees did not pollinate apple blossoms, we would not have apples. Bees and wasps pollinate many other plants as well.

108:   No, spiders are not insects. Count their legs. Spiders belong to a family called Arachnids.

109:   Earthworms help to enrich the soil. Also by tunneling under the soil, they mix and loosen the soil. This lets air into the ground. The air is good for plant roots.

110:   The light colors are easier to see in the dark and the sweet smell is often stronger at night. Light colors and strong scents attract moths and other insects that pollinate the flowers.

111:   Moving air forces the blades of the windmill to turn.

112:   You can measure around the trunk. This will tell you about how old the tree is. If the tree has been cut down, you can count the rings on the stump. Trees grow a new ring every year.

113:   The air over the lamp is warm. The balloon will rise with the warm air, but will sink as soon as it drifts into cooler air.

114:   Roots could be carrot sticks or potatoes, seeds could be peanuts or beans or rice, berries could be strawberries, blueberries, or cranberries

115:   When you speak into the cup, it vibrates with your voice. The cup makes the string vibrate and it carries the vibrations to the cup on the other end. The string makes the other cup vibrate and you hear the voice on the other end.

116:   The chemicals and nutrients in dead materials are used over and over again. If dead material did not break down, waste would pile up on the earth.

117:   You could change the center of gravity. You can do this by making your end of the seesaw longer and your friend's shorter. You could also ask another friend to sit with you. What might happen then?

118: The kittens are learning how to protect themselves from larger animals. They are also learning skills that will help them catch mice!

119: Rice, wheat, corn, and oats are all plants from the grass family. Think about this when you choose your breakfast cereal!

120: Most minerals are made from one substance and many have crystals. Some of the minerals that you may see everyday are things such as table salt, pencil lead (graphite), glass (silica), and diamonds. Rocks may have several minerals in them, depending on how they were formed.

121: You would be older if you lived on Mercury, because the years are shorter than they are on Earth. Your birthday would come every 88 days.

122: Animals that get milk from their mothers are mammals.

123: Wallabies, which are the smallest kangaroos, are about one foot high and weigh up to 3 pounds.

124: Cuttings are pieces of a plant, such as an African violet leaf with its stalk, or a leafy stem from an ivy or coleus. Fill a small jar or glass half full with water, and prop the cutting in the jar. Roots will grow from the stem.

125: People have used two kinds of language to talk to chimpanzees. Sign language (ameslan) is the same language hearing-impaired people use. The other language is yerkish. This is a language that uses a special computer keyboard. Chimpanzees can use the keyboard to talk to people.

126: Sharks have cartilage, which is like the tissue in your nose or your ear. But in sharks it is harder and stronger. It almost feels like bone.

127: All of these thing are levers! Levers have three parts. A fulcrum is the spot where the lever pivots. You push down or lift up to make the force. The load works in the opposite direction to the force.

128: The mantis eats many insect pests. Its big eyes help it spot caterpillars and beetles that could harm your garden. It is always hungry and has lots of babies who are also hungry!

129: It would take about ten years to walk to the moon. The *Apollo* spaceships took three days to reach the moon.

130: Electric eels can produce up to 600 volts of electricity. This is enough to kill a large animal.

131: There are minerals in the water that the fish, snails, and mussels can break down into food. In addition, some food falls down from the lighted zone above.

132: You probably live in a moderate climate. Moderate climates have seasons that change from winter to spring, from spring to summer, and from summer to fall and then back to winter.

133: Dragonflies hunt mosquitoes and other small insects! They can bend their legs into a kind of basket shape. They swoop down and capture mosquitoes with this basket.

134: Red and green colors are easier for your eyes to see in poor light. Blue and purple are harder to tell apart and harder to see in dim light.

135: The gray toad is the same toad as the green toad. Tree toads can change their colors to match what they are resting on.

136: The mammal is an elephant seal. It grows to be twenty feet long and may weigh as much as three tons. Elephant seals do not live in the water all the time.

137: Humpback whales sing, and they change their songs from year to year. All the whales in one group sing the same song. Whale groups in different parts of the world sing different songs.

138: The outer covering of a snake's body is always being worn by friction as it crawls and doesn't stretch or grow the way your skin does. When a snake sheds its skin, it even sheds the part that covers its eyes!

139: Smog is smoke and fumes that mix with moisture in the air. You can see smog. It looks like a dirty brown cloud.

140: A pupa is the insect, a cocoon is a covering made by the insect. Cocoons are usually made from materials such as leaves or tiny twigs and silk from the insect's body. Cocoons protect pupas from harm and the weather. Some pupas spend the winter in a cocoon. When a butterfly hatches directly from a pupa, it is like shedding the skin.

141: The cars rolled down the ramp because of gravity.

142: They noticed that the planets reflected light. The light could only come from the sun. If they traveled around the Earth, they would not reflect sunlight in the same way.

143: Shark's teeth are arranged in many rows. If they lose one, a new tooth from another row moves into its place.

144: Most tea kettles that whistle do so because hot water expands and produces steam. The steam expands and pushes air and steam through the whistle, making the sound.

145: The soil is warmed by the sun. Some alligators pile decaying plants over the eggs they lay. Heat from the plants warms the eggs.

146: Yes. The moon orbits the Earth. But the Earth and the moon together orbit the sun. Some of the other planets have moons that also orbit their planets. The planets and their moons orbit the sun together.

147: Silk comes from fibers spun by silkworms, an insect larva. The silkworms produce long fibers when they make their cocoons. Each worm can make about 915 meters (1,000 yards) of thread.

148: The plants bend toward the light. The cells on the dark side of the plant grow longer than those on the light side. This makes the plant grow toward light. This property is called heliotropism.

149: Fireflies are actually a kind of beetle. They use their flashing lights to attract mates.

150: What looks like a falling star is probably a piece of rock called a meteor. When meteors enter Earth's atmosphere, they are traveling very fast. They get so hot that they glow! Most of them burn up before they reach the ground.

151: Spots and stripes help change the animal's appearance, and it can hide from enemies. Most animals do not see color, and these patterns help the animal hide against a background of leaves and trunks. Looking like a leaf or a twig helps insects to escape being noticed by hungry birds and animals!

152: It evaporated. When water evaporates it goes into the air.

153: Even in the summer, the sun's rays are too weak to raise the temperature enough to melt the snow. For many months of the year, the sunlight doesn't even reach the poles!

154: Water could make large wheels turn. The turning wheels made machinery move. Some of the machines would grind wheat or corn for flour. Some machines helped to spin thread and weave cloth. Some helped saw wood into lumber. We use water power today to make electricity.

155: You can do this without a friend too. Just sit quietly in your house and listen.

156: Some wasps may use mud to build cells for their eggs. Other wasps build homes of paper. They make the paper from bits of chewed leaves, rotting wood, and plant stems.

157: Dolphins communicate with each other using special sounds. For example, certain sounds mean danger and others are cries for help. Trained dolphins have learned that whistles can carry messages. They have helped divers locate objects underwater.

158: Many insects such as grasshoppers have more than two eyes. They also have eyes with many lenses. What an insect sees probably looks like a picture made of many little pieces. Eyes like this are good at detecting motion and help protect the insect from being caught and eaten!

159: Molars and premolars, at the back of your mouth, grind food. Your front teeth, canines and incisors, are for biting and cutting food.

160: Melted rock is called lava or magma. It flows down the side of the volcano.

161: The sun had melted the snow a little. When it got cold at night, the melted snow turned to ice. Ice has less friction than snow, so the sleds went faster.

162: Hummingbirds don't need big heavy bones. Their bones need to be light, strong, and tiny so they can fly easily. Bones of a heavy animal like an elephant are thick and solid while a hummingbird's bones are thin and hollow.

163: The water held the sand together in the shapes of towers and walls. When the water evaporated, the sand collapsed.

164: The octopus has eight arms. (*Octo* means eight.) If one arm is chopped off, it will grow a new arm.

165: The medicine is penicillin. It was discovered by Dr. Alexander Fleming in 1928. Penicillin kills many dangerous bacteria that cause illness.

166: They can be grown in water-soaked sand or gravel or just water alone. This is called hydroponics. Some kinds of vegetables, such as tomatoes and lettuce, are grown this way. Plant food mixed in the water helps them grow big and strong.

167: No. Rabbits have eyes on the sides of their faces. They need to be able to watch in two directions for their enemies, because they are prey.

168: Your tongue has a sense of touch.

169: Noon. It would be mid-day and the sun would be directly overhead.

170: Birds sing to warn other birds to stay away. When they sing, they are saying, "This is my area. The space here belongs to me." This space is called the bird's territory.

171: The yucca moth pollinates the flowers of the yucca plant. The yucca plant produces seeds that the yucca moth caterpillars eat. There are many seeds and some are left uneaten and grow into new yucca plants.

172: When the air is damp, the cones will close up tight. When it is dry, they open wide.

173: The other colors are combinations of these three colors along with white. The dots that are combined are too small to be seen and your eyes and brain are fooled into believing that they see the other colors!

174: Turtles do not have lips or teeth! Instead, their jaws have sharp edges and are shaped like beaks. They are able to bite off bits of grass and leaves, or tear apart small fish with this sharp beak. Turtles do have tongues which help them to swallow.

175: Plants give off oxygen. Fish need oxygen to breathe. Even though there is oxygen in the water, it is good to increase the oxygen supply. Plants also provide a place for fish to hide.

176: Yes, earthworms can live if they are chopped in two. They have a nervous system that is spread along the length of their bodies. The nervous system takes the place of a brain. Earthworms can even grow new parts if less than half of the body is lost.

177: Sponges are actually animals. They have no legs, fins, or stomachs. Sponges get food by pumping water through small openings in their bodies. Natural sponges that you buy are the skeletons of these animals.

178: In the fall, cells develop across the leaf stem. They block the flow of water to the leaf. The green chlorophyll disappears and other colors in the leaf that were covered by the green appear.

179: On Jupiter because it has a larger mass

180: About 179 days, almost half a year